Living in Trees

by Alexandra Behr

HOUGHTON MIFFLIN HARCOURT
School Publishers

ILLUSTRATION CREDIT: Joe LeMonnier

PHOTOGRAPHY CREDITS: Cover © Anders Ryman / Alamy. 1 © Getty Images. 2 © Getty Images. 4 © Anders Ryman/ Alamy. 5 © Digital Stock. 6 © Corbis. 7 Marjorie C. Leggitt. 8 © Jim Zuckerman/Corbis. 9 © Digital Stock. 10 Mark Moffett/Minden Pictures. 11 Mark Moffett/Minden Pictures. 12 © Digital Vision. 13 © Hornbil Image /Alamy. 14 Associated Press.

Printed in China

ISBN-13: 978-0-547-01741-9
ISBN-10: 0-547-01741-3

5 6 7 8 0940 18 17 16 15 14 13 12
4500351837

You walk through a city park. Above, in the trees, you see sunlight sifting through the leaves. Then you see a tree house that someone has made in one of the trees.

You quickly climb the ladder. Standing on the tree house floor, you look down upon the whole park. You hear the constant singing of the birds in the branches around you. If only you could live in a tree house like this right now!

Impossible? Well, maybe not. Some people actually do live and work in tree houses in regions all over the world.

Papua New Guinea

Equator

Life in a Tree House

Imagine that you are canoeing through a swampy wilderness in Papua New Guinea (PA poo ah noo GIN ee), a country near Australia. You are going to meet a group of native people called the Kombai. The Kombai live in small communities, far from the island's cities.

The Kombai build their homes in trees in the forest. That's a cool idea, you think. But the Kombai don't build their tree houses because they think they're cool. Their tree houses protect them from floods and give them shelter from the heat and insects down below. Living above the ground also protects the Kombai from unwanted visitors—animal or human!

Kombai tree houses are built as high as 100 feet above the ground.

The Kombai use local resources in the forest for their homes, household items, and clothing. They cut down trees with stone axes and slice food with sharp pieces of bamboo. They weave palm leaves into skirts. Their lightweight clothing keeps them from getting overheated.

The climate in Papua New Guinea is very rainy. So don't be surprised if a thunderstorm dumps buckets of rain on you. Luckily, a tree house is nearby. You climb the ladder and join a family for their meal—wild boar and some of the starchy food the Kombai make from palm trees. Then you can munch on an unexpected Kombai treat—the worm-like larvae of Capricorn beetles.

One palm tree can supply a Kombai family with enough food for about 7 to 10 days. So what happens when all the palms are cut down and used for food? The Kombai family then has to move to a new part of the forest. Then it will be time to build another tree house high above the ground!

Work in a Tree House

Now imagine that you are hiking through a tropical rainforest in Central America. The weather feels muggy. Bugs are bugging you! As you take photos of the lush green trees, you wonder, is someone watching you?

You might guess it's a spider monkey… a tree frog… a parrot… a colony of ants… or perhaps a snake, quietly waiting.

Would you be surprised to find out that a scientist is looking down at you, too? In some rainforests, scientists work in special tree houses high above the rainforest floor. From there they study one of the most interesting habitats on Earth.

Canopy

Understory

Floor

The layers of the rainforest

Rainforests have several layers. The bottom layer is the forest floor. It is covered with fallen leaves and small twigs. Little sunlight reaches this level. Down there, you might see a strange-looking tapir nibbling on plants…. Or a scary jaguar looking for a tasty tapir!

The next layer is called the understory. It contains young trees with thin trunks and large leaves. Snakes, frogs, butterflies, insects, and birds live in this layer.

Many scientists have wished for a bird's-eye view of the
rainforest canopy.

The canopy is the layer that is formed by the
leaves and branches of the rainforest's tallest trees.
It is usually more than 80 feet above the forest floor.
Sometimes it can be as high as 200 feet!

Because it's so high up, the canopy gets lots of
sun and rain. That's how it produces so many seeds,
fruits, leaves, flowers, and nuts. All this food makes it a
place where many animals can live. In fact, most of the
animals in the rainforest live in the canopy.

The canopy is the heart of the rainforest because it is home to so many kinds of animals and plants. In some rainforests, monkeys swing on branches and vines that form a sort of canopy highway. In others, you might find flying lemurs, flying squirrels, frogs, and other creatures leaping and gliding from one tree to another. Birds, bats, snakes, and bugs all keep the canopy buzzing with life.

Scientists have long wanted to study the canopy's rich life. But because the canopy is so high above the forest floor, they have not been able to figure out how to study it. In the past, scientists have cut down trees to study what lives in the treetops. They have used ropes to climb up the trees. One scientist even trained a monkey to bring him samples of plants from the canopy!

This canopy raft and hot air balloon were used to study the canopy of a rainforest in Africa.

Today, scientists have found new ways to study the canopy for long periods of time. They climb spiral staircases or use cranes to carry them to tree house camps high above the rainforest floor. They walk through the canopy on walkways that are tied from tree to tree. Some scientists even use hot air balloons to carry them to the treetops.

A canopy crane in an Australian rainforest rises almost 160 feet in the air. Its long arm reaches over the trees. The crane helps scientists observe the animals and plants in the hard-to-reach canopy.

Scientists in Panama use two tower cranes to study the rainforest there. You've probably seen tower cranes being used to build city skyscrapers and other tall buildings. Researchers are lifted from the ground in cars that swing out over the rainforest from the crane's arm. The researchers communicate with the crane operator using radios. The crane operator moves the researchers to different places in the canopy where they can study for hours.

Researchers study the Panama rainforest from a car held up by a tower crane.

Play in a Tree House

Okay, you're tired of canoeing through swamps.... And studying the canopy of the rainforest has exhausted you. Now you just want to relax. What better place to do that than in one of these amazing tree house hotels?

A tree house hotel in South Africa has a wonderful view of the forest and a nearby gorge. If you're more interested in seeing wild animals, there's a tree house hotel in Kenya near a wildlife reserve full of protected animals.

This tree house hotel in India lets visitors sleep close to nature.

At one tree house resort in India, you have to climb across rope bridges to get to your treetop hotel room. Stepping out on a balcony, you can see animals such as monkeys, birds, or even elephants.

But if India is too far from your home, you might want to visit the tree house hotel on Mount Rainier. It's in the state of Washington. Your room is 50 feet from the ground of the forest. A bridge connects the tree house to an observatory that's even higher. Imagine what you can see from there!

Tree Houses for Everyone

You have seen that tree houses can be used for many reasons. But maybe the best reason to use a tree house is to have fun. That's what kids do if they have the good luck to live near a tree house.

But tree houses are not just for kids who can easily climb. There's a company that builds tree houses for kids who are ill or have disabilities that make climbing difficult. These tree houses have ramps and walkways. Even kids who use wheelchairs and walkers can climb into these tree houses.

That way, everyone has fun.

This tree house was built especially for children with special needs.

Responding

Main Idea and Details

The Kombai use local resources for many needs. What details support this main idea? Copy and complete the chart below.

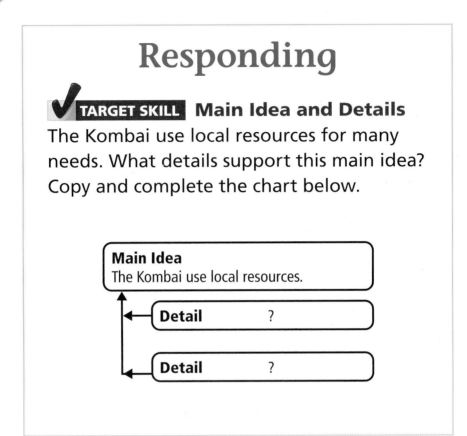

Main Idea
The Kombai use local resources.

Detail ?

Detail ?

✎ Write About It

Text to World Write a paragraph to persuade your community that your town needs a tree house in one of its parks. Include answers to objections that people might have, along with your reasons.

✔ **TARGET SKILL** **Main Ideas and Details** Tell important ideas and details about a topic.

✔ **TARGET STRATEGY** **Infer/Predict** Use clues to figure out more about the selection.

GENRE **Informational text** gives factual information about a topic.